THE RESTORATION OF DIVINE ORDER

BOOK THREE

Patterns, Discernment, and the Final Return of the King

Michael A. Kovach

The Restoration of Divine Order Press

I0203046

Copyright

The Restoration of Divine Order, Book Three

Published by Covenant Light Publishing
(Restoration of Divine Order Press)
Jacksonville, Florida

Unless otherwise indicated:

Old Testament quotations are from the **New King James Version (NKJV).**
New Testament quotations are from the **New American Standard Bible 1995 (NASB95).**

Cover design by: *[Michael A. Kovach*
Interior design by: *[Michael A. Kovach*

ISBN (Paperback): 979-8-9940916-0-9

Printed in the United States of America.

Dedication

To the glory of God, and to all who seek His order, His peace, and their rightful place in Christ's Kingdom.

To my pastor, who set me on a path of deeper study through faithful instruction, challenge, and entrusted assignments.

To my wife, whose unwavering encouragement and quiet strength have sustained this calling.

To my Sunday study group, whose hunger for truth stirred me not only to teach, but to write.

To the many individuals whose gifts in programming and technology created the tools that supported this work.

And to every extraordinary person the Lord placed along my path — thank you for your influence, friendship, and faithfulness.

Acknowledgments

Every work is shaped by the people God places in our lives.
This book, and the trilogy it completes, is no exception.

I thank my pastor for his challenging questions, faithful guidance, and his insistence that Scripture must shape not only our thinking but our living.

I thank my wife, whose steadfast support enabled me to devote the time, focus, and prayer needed to complete these volumes.

I thank my Sunday study group, who listened, wrestled, discussed, and sharpened ideas long before they reached these pages.

I thank the technologists, programmers, and engineers whose creativity produced the tools that enabled this work to be written, edited, organized, and prepared for publication.

Most of all, I thank the Lord, whose patience, correction, mercy, and steadfast love guided every line.

Preface

A Season of Clarity After a Lifetime of Seeking

Every book is born from a moment. This book, however, was born over the course of decades.

For most of my life, I carried insights that felt significant but incomplete— threads of understanding that surfaced early in my walk with God, resurfaced through years of teaching, and matured through seasons of trial, prayer, and revelation. What I did not realize then was that each insight, each burden, each awakening was part of a much larger pattern the Spirit was slowly revealing.

Books One and Two laid the foundation for understanding this pattern.

Book One explored Divine Order as the framework of creation — the structural, relational, and covenantal design woven into everything God made.

Book Two exposed the consequences of disorder — how drift fractures identity, distorts relationships, weakens covenant, and reshapes the world around us.

For years, these two themes formed the outer edges of a larger picture. Book Three brings that picture into focus.

This volume is not simply a continuation—it is the culmination of what God has been teaching me over a lifetime of discipleship. It reflects decades of reading Scripture, wrestling with truth, confronting personal drift, teaching others, and walking with countless believers through their own struggles.

More importantly, this book is written for a moment such as this — a moment when the world is shaking, the church is shifting, and believers are seeking clarity amid confusion. The patterns described in these chapters are not theoretical; they are visible in the world around us, in the culture we inhabit, and sometimes even in the quiet corners of our own hearts.

If you have read the first two books, you will recognize familiar themes. But Book Three goes deeper — into the cultural, spiritual, and personal patterns that reveal why Divine Order matters now more than ever.

It also reveals something essential: What God forms across decades, He clarifies in His time.

My prayer is that these chapters help you recognize what the Spirit is revealing in this generation, and what He is restoring in the hearts of His people. These pages were written with humility, reflection, and a deep sense of responsibility — not to add noise to the world, but to call attention to what God is already doing.

Thank you for joining me on this journey. May these words strengthen your walk, deepen your discernment, and draw your heart into closer alignment with the One who orders all things. —*M.A.K.*

Table of Contents

FOREWORD

There are moments in history when God calls His people to see more clearly than they ever have before. Moments when culture shifts beneath our feet, when familiar landmarks disappear, when institutions tremble, and when believers sense—deep in the Spirit—that something far greater is happening beneath the surface.

We are living in such a moment.

For decades, many have felt a quiet stirring, a spiritual unease, an awareness that the world we once knew is no longer the world we are walking in. The foundations that shaped our faith communities, families, and identity are being shaken. Confusion is celebrated as enlightenment. Disorder is labeled as progress. Truth is treated as negotiable. Discernment is dismissed as intolerance. And many Christians—earnest, sincere, well-intentioned—find themselves unsure how to stand, interpret the times, or navigate the growing tensions around them.

This is precisely why The Restoration of Divine Order: Book 3 exists.

This volume does not merely analyze culture or critique the modern church. Many books do that. What this book does is far more urgent and far more rare: **it teaches believers to see the patterns of Divine Order and disorder unfolding across time, history, nations, churches, and the human heart.**

The author has spent more than forty years studying Scripture, teaching believers, ministering in diverse contexts, and writing hundreds of essays. Yet the insights found in these pages did not emerge from academic theory—they were forged through decades of experience, prayer, struggle, revelation, and obedience.

Book One uncovers the architecture of God's order woven into creation and covenant.

Book Two exposes the tensions, fractures, and relational dynamics that distort that order.

Book Three reveals the pattern behind it all:

- Why cultures collapse.
- Why churches drift.
- Why believers struggle.
- Why discernment falters.
- Why the will fails when the Spirit must prevail.
- Why God is calling His people back into alignment.
- Why Christ's return is not only inevitable but near.

This book helps readers stop seeing life as a series of isolated moments and start recognizing the spiritual patterns that shape everything around them. It trains the believer not merely to react to the world but to interpret it—to see what God sees, discern what God reveals, and walk in the order God designed.

More importantly, this book extends hope.

It reminds us that disorder is not the final word. Christ is.

It reminds us that God exposes disorder not to shame us, but to restore us. He shakes what can be shaken so that what is unshakable may remain.

It reminds us that the Spirit is still forming a people who will stand with clarity, courage, and conviction in the days ahead—not by human strength, but by divine alignment.

These chapters encourage you to reflect on both your surroundings and you, assuring that God restores all who return to His design.

This book is a gift to the Body of Christ. It is both a warning and an encouragement. Both a diagnosis and a roadmap. Both a reflection on what has been and a preparation for what is coming.

May you read these pages slowly. May you read them prayerfully. May you allow the Spirit to illuminate what you have not seen, align what has drifted, and strengthen what has weakened.

The days ahead will require believers who walk not in confusion, but in Divine Order, not in fear, but in discernment, not in cultural imitation, but in spiritual authority.

You hold in your hands a book that will help you become such a believer.

May the Spirit guide you; may Christ anchor you, and may the Father restore in you everything He intended from the beginning.

CHAPTER ONE - Prologue

Seeing the Whole Story ▪ How God Reveals Order Through Time

_____

"What God reveals across decades becomes clear only when the Spirit gives us the eyes to see the pattern."

"Divine Order is not discovered in a moment—it is revealed through a lifetime of God's faithful shaping."

Every story God writes unfolds slowly. We rarely see its fullness while we are living it. Instead, we experience it moment by moment, year by year, revelation by revelation. And only later — sometimes much later — do we recognize the pattern, the meaning, and the purpose woven through it.

Book 3 exists because of that kind of hindsight.

What began as separate reflections written across decades — comments on culture, warnings to the church, meditations on the inner life, notes scribbled in margins, studies shared with believers hungry for truth — were not isolated teachings. They were early signals of a larger revelation God was forming in me long before I had the language for it.

This final volume is not simply "the next book."
It is the lens through which the first two books come into focus.

Book One traced the architecture of Divine Order — the design God built into creation, covenant, identity, and kingdom life.

Book Two revealed the relational tensions that disturb that order in families, churches, communities, and generations.

But Book Three explains why these insights matter now, and how God was preparing this framework through a lifetime of experiences.

Because Divine Order does not exist only in theology — it exists in history.
It does not appear only in doctrines — it appears in the patterns of life.
It is not merely an idea — it is a revelation unfolding across time.

The Gift of Retrospective Revelation

We often hear God clearly only after the echoes fade.
Something he spoke years ago suddenly makes sense.
A burden we carried in a past season becomes relevant again.
A question we asked long ago finds its answer in a moment of spiritual clarity.

This book is born from that reality.

Decades ago, when I wrote about cultural decline, about the confusion of the will, about the drift of the modern church, about the urgency of returning to genuine discipleship — I only saw symptoms, not the full story.

Now, after years of prayer, teaching, reflection, and study, I see the pattern:

Where Divine Order is abandoned, disorder multiplies.
Where Divine Order is embraced, restoration begins.

This truth threads its way through every chapter that follows.

Why Book 3 Needed to Be Written

Many books analyze culture.
Many critique the church.
Many explore spiritual formation.
Many warn of the last days.

But Book Three does something different:

It reveals how all these worlds collide when Divine Order is lost—and how they are restored when God's order returns.

This volume answers the more profound questions:

Michael A. Kovach

- Why does the world look the way it does today?
- Why is the modern church struggling with clarity and courage?
- Why do believers feel spiritually conflicted, exhausted, or directionless?
- Why does disorder manifest the same patterns across generations?
- How does the Spirit bring restoration in these last days?
- What has God been showing us that we failed to understand?

These questions are not philosophical — they are pastoral.
They are personal.
They are urgent.

Book Three is a call to wake up, to see clearly, to stand faithfully, and to walk in alignment with God in a world steadily drifting into confusion.

The Missing Piece: Pattern Recognition

This is the contribution Book 3 makes to the trilogy:

It teaches us how to recognize the patterns of Divine Order and disorder across time.

Pattern recognition allows the believer to see:

- Why cultures collapse
- Why churches compromise
- Why Believers Drift
- Why deception spreads
- Why fear dominates
- Why the truth is resisted
- Why the Spirit calls us back to obedience
- Why Christ will soon return to restore all things

This is not pessimism — it is clarity.
It is seeing what God sees.
It is interpreting history through the eyes of Scripture.
It is connecting the dots between yesterday and today.

Because once we see the pattern, we know how to walk in the path God designed.

How This Book Is Structured

Book Three unfolds in movements, each one revealing another layer of Divine Order:

Chapters 2–4: The World's Disorder

Cultural drift, loss of discernment, and the collapse of moral identity.

Chapters 5–7: The Church's Disorder

Counterfeit Christianity, selective obedience, and the cost of authentic discipleship.

Chapters 8–11: The Believer's Disorder

The tension between will and flesh, spiritual confusion, blind spots, and inward resistance.

Chapters 12–14: The Revelation and Restoration of Order

Pattern recognition, pathways of restoration, and the coming return of Christ.

Every section leads the reader from clarity → to conviction → to transformation → to hope.

We do not merely identify disorder—we show the path back to Divine Order.

A Personal Word Before We Begin

What you are about to read is not academic.
It is not a theory.
It is not a compilation of random essays.
It is the testimony of decades—the record of what God was shaping in me long before I knew its purpose.

My prayer is that as you read, the Spirit will open your eyes to the same patterns He opened in mine:

- where disorder has entered your life

Michael A. Kovach

- where God is calling you into surrender
- where clarity needs to replace confusion
- where obedience needs to replace hesitation
- where hope needs to replace fear
- where Divine Order needs to be restored

And that through this process, you will walk more confidently, more joyfully, and more courageously in the days ahead.

Because we are approaching a time when only those who walk in Divine Order — under the authority of Christ, empowered by the Spirit, anchored in Scripture, and purified in heart — will stand firm.

This book was written to help you stand.

CHAPTER TWO

What Is Happening to Us? — A Nation Losing Its Memory of Itself

---

"Cultures collapse publicly only after they have collapsed privately."

"Disorder always begins in the heart before it appears in the nation."

A Nation Losing Its Memory of Itself

Every generation reaches a moment when it must face the truth about itself. Not the truth of what it wants to be, not the truth of what it pretends to be, but the reality of **what it has become.**

We are living in a time when societies—especially those shaped by centuries of biblical influence—are losing their memory of the very foundations that once gave them stability, identity, and moral clarity.

Disorder does not appear suddenly.
It emerges gradually, quietly, and predictably.
It appears first in the **heart**, then in the **home**, then in the **church**, and finally in the **nation**.

What we are witnessing today is not an isolated cultural shift, but a **pattern repeated throughout history** whenever people drift from the One who establishes order.

This chapter is not political.

It is spiritual.
It is diagnostic.
It is a sober attempt to answer the question many believers are quietly asking:

"What is happening to us?"

Michael A. Kovach

We Are Watching a Slow Erosion of Moral Clarity

The first sign of cultural decline is not lawlessness on the streets—it is lawlessness in the heart.

A culture begins to lose itself when it:

1. Elevates personal preference above objective truth
2. Redefines right and wrong
3. Dismisses the authority of Scripture
4. Mocks holiness
5. Celebrates rebellion
6. Silences conviction

This erosion is subtle at first. It begins with confusion, not chaos.

- Questions become louder than convictions.
- Feelings become louder than Scripture.
- Experience becomes louder than truth.

And once clarity is lost, disorder begins.

We Have Traded Truth for Narratives

Truth has become optional in the modern world.
Narratives—polished, emotional, persuasive stories—have become the new currency of public life.

But narratives do not need to be true to be effective.

A narrative only needs:

1. Repetition
2. Emotion
3. Acceptance
4. Amplification

The serpent deceived Eve not with power, but with narrative.

When truth becomes negotiable, discernment becomes unnecessary, and deception becomes inevitable.

We Are Witnessing the Collapse of Discernment

Discernment is the ability to distinguish between what is right and what merely sounds right, between what is good and what feels good. Between what is holy and what is fashionable.

Discernment requires:

1. A submitted heart
2. A renewed mind
3. A reverent fear of the Lord
4. A clear moral compass
5. The anchoring of Scripture
6. Humility before God

When these fade, discernment collapses.

And without discernment, a nation becomes vulnerable to every wind of doctrine, every cultural trend, every ideological shift, and every deceptive Spirit that promises freedom while delivering bondage.

Paul warned about this long ago:

"… tossed here and there by waves and carried about by every wind of doctrine…"
(Ephesians 4:14, NASB95)

This is not just a church problem—it is a cultural one.

We Have Replaced Conviction With Comfort

Conviction leads to repentance.

Comfort leads to complacency.

Michael A. Kovach

A nation that prioritizes comfort will never stand on conviction.
It will always trade truth for convenience.

We see this in:

1. Entertainment that numbs the conscience
2. Technology that distracts from holiness
3. Institutions that reward compromise
4. Leaders who avoid conflict
5. Churches that choose popularity over purity

When comfort becomes the highest virtue, holiness becomes optional.

A comfortable person cannot carry a cross.

We Are Losing the Fear of God

At the root of every collapse—personal, ecclesial, or national—is the loss of the fear of the Lord.

Scripture says:

"The fear of the Lord is the beginning of wisdom."
(Proverbs 9:10, NKJV)

Without fear of God:

1. Wisdom collapses
2. Truth collapses
3. Discernment collapses
4. Moral courage collapses
5. Spiritual vitality collapses

A nation that no longer fears God will eventually fear everything else.

Fear of man.
Fear of loss.
Fear of rejection.
Fear of being on the wrong side of culture.

Fear becomes the new master.
And it is a cruel one.

We Are Seeing the Fruit of Generational Drift

Drift does not begin with rebellion;
it begins with neglect.

One generation tolerates what the previous one rejected.
The next embraces what the previous tolerated.

Eventually, children forget their grandparents' convictions, question their parents' convictions, and abandon their faith's convictions.

Cultural drift is generational. But so is revival.

Witnessing the Consequences of Abandoning Divine Order

Disorder is not merely political or social—it is spiritual.

When Divine Order is abandoned:

1.   Identity becomes confused
2.   Morality becomes subjective
3.   Institutions become unstable
4.   Relationships fracture
5.   Families weaken
6.   Churches compromise
7.   Deception spreads
8.   Fear increases
9.   Hope diminishes

This is not a coincidence.
It is the predictable outcome of departing from God's design.

Order is not the enemy of freedom—it is the foundation of it.

Michael A. Kovach
So, What Is Happening to Us?

We are living through the consequences of:

1. losing our moral compass
2. losing our discernment
3. losing our reverence
4. losing our courage
5. losing our memory of God

But here is the hope:

When God exposes disorder, He is preparing the way for restoration.

This exposure is mercy.
This shaking is grace.
This disruption is preparation.

Because God always reveals the brokenness before He restores the order.

The Next Step: Understanding the Pattern

Chapter 2 diagnoses the condition.
Chapter 3 (next) explains **how discernment dies**, and how the enemy uses confusion to blind nations, churches, and believers.

Then Book Three progresses deeper:

1. from culture
2. to institutions
3. to the church
4. to the believer
5. to the revelation of Divine Order
6. to the restoration Christ brings at His return

This is not just cultural commentary—it is preparation for the days ahead.

Conclusion:

What is happening to us is not new.
It is a pattern.
It is ancient.
It is predictable.
It is spiritual.
It is the same path walked by every nation that forgets God.

But God is not done.
He is revealing, shaking, exposing, and preparing.
He is calling His people to see clearly again.
To walk in truth again.
To fear Him again.
To live in His order again.

And this book exists to help His people do exactly that.

Michael A. Kovach
CHAPTER THREE

The Loss of Discernment in Modern Culture — When Light and Darkness Become Indistinguishable.

_____

"A culture without discernment becomes a culture without truth."

"The greatest danger to the church is not darkness—it is when light becomes indistinguishable from darkness."

How a Nation Forgets the Difference Between Light and Darkness

Discernment is one of the first casualties of cultural decline.

Long before a nation collapses morally, economically, or socially, it collapses spiritually — and the clearest indicator of spiritual collapse is **the loss of discernment**.

Discernment is not suspicion.
It is not intuition.
It is not cynicism.
Discernment is **the ability to distinguish between truth and error, wisdom and foolishness, righteousness and wickedness, God's voice and every other voice.**

Without discernment, people cannot tell the difference between what heals and what destroys, what is holy and what is profane, what is eternal and what is temporary, what is good and what merely feels good.

The prophet Isaiah warned of such a time:

"Woe to those who call evil good, and good evil;
Who substitute darkness for light and light for darkness."
— Isaiah 5:20 (NKJV)

That warning was not written for pagans —it was addressed to God's covenant people.

It is possible to become so desensitized, so unmoored, so influenced by the world's narrative that even believers begin to mistake darkness for light.

This is the crisis of discernment in the modern age.

How Discernment Dies

Discernment does not disappear instantly. It erodes gradually through four predictable stages — stages we now see unfolding across our society.

Stage 1: Replacing Revelation With Emotion

When a culture begins trusting feelings more than truth, discernment weakens.
Emotion becomes the new authority.
Experience becomes the new morality.
Sincerity becomes the new holiness.

But sincerity without truth is still deception.

Stage 2: Replacing Obedience With Autonomy

When obedience becomes optional, morality becomes negotiable.
People begin to assume they are the final arbiters of right and wrong.

Autonomy may feel empowering, but it is spiritually blinding.

Stage 3: Replacing Wisdom With Information

We have more information than any generation before us — and less wisdom.
Information does not shape virtue.
Information does not purify motives.
Information does not anchor the soul.

The internet gives data; only God gives discernment.

Stage 4: Replacing Holiness With Tolerance

Michael A. Kovach

Our culture has redefined love as affirmation and holiness as cruelty.
When holiness becomes offensive, discernment collapses.

A culture without holiness cannot discern what is sacred.

The Quiet Power of Cultural Catechism

Every culture catechizes its people — not through classrooms but through:

1. Entertainment
2. News cycles
3. Slogans
4. Symbols
5. Humor
6. Expectations
7. Social pressure
8. Repeated messaging

Culture shapes the heart like water shapes stone — slowly, repeatedly, invisibly.

Without discernment, believers become disciples of the age rather than disciples of Christ.

Paul warns:

"Do not be conformed to this world, but be transformed by the renewing of your mind."— Romans 12:2 (NASB95)

Conformity is subtle.
It arrives disguised as relevance.
It grows through compromise.
It thrives in the absence of conviction.

The Role of Fear in the Loss of Discernment

Fear suffocates discernment by forcing silence.

People no longer say what is true; they say what is *safe*.
People no longer defend righteousness; they defend reputations.
People no longer speak from conviction; they speak from caution.

Fear of man produces compromise.
Fear of God produces clarity.

Where discernment is absent, fear has taken its place.

The Seduction of Half-Truths

The greatest threat to discernment is not blatant lies —it is **half-truths**.

Half-truths:

1. Sound moral
2. Feel compassionate
3. Appear wise
4. Seem harmless
5. Use Scripture selectively

But half-truths divorce holiness from love, obedience from faith, and righteousness from compassion.

Paul warned:

"Satan disguises himself as an angel of light."
— 2 Corinthians 11:14 (NASB95)

Deception is most effective when it looks holy.

The Consequences of a Culture Without Discernment

When discernment collapses, a nation begins to:

1. Redefine sin
2. Avoid correction

Michael A. Kovach

3.   Resist truth
4.   Celebrate rebellion
5.   Mock righteousness
6.   Devalue life
7.   Weaponize identity
8.   Polarize morality
9.   Trust experts over Scripture
10.   Prefer charisma to character

This is not merely moral decline —it is **spiritual blindness**.

And the deeper tragedy is this:

A culture without discernment produces a church without discernment.

The Last Days Demand Discernment

Paul's warnings to Timothy describe our modern moment with stunning accuracy:

1.   lovers of self
2.   lovers of pleasure
3.   holding to a form of godliness
4.   always learning but never arriving at truth
        (2 Timothy 3:1–7)

Discernment is no longer optional; it is essential for survival.

The believer who lacks discernment will drift.
The believer who walks in discernment will stand.

Discernment is the difference between being deceived and being delivered.

Restoring Discernment Begins With Returning to Divine Order

Discernment is restored when:

1. Scripture reclaims authority
2. Obedience replaces preference
3. Holiness replaces permissiveness
4. truth replaces emotion
5. Repentance replaces defensiveness
6. Humility replaces pride
7. The fear of God replaces fear of man

The Spirit restores discernment in those who submit to truth.

Conclusion:

A culture without discernment is a culture ripe for deception.
A believer without discernment is a believer vulnerable to compromise.
But a church walking in discernment becomes a light in a world that has forgotten what light looks like.

Discernment is not a spiritual luxury. It is spiritual survival.

And this chapter prepares the ground for Chapter 4 — a deeper examination of how disorder infiltrates institutions, families, churches, and nations.

CHAPTER FOUR

How Disorder Enters Institutions ▬ When Structures Drift From God's Design.

"Institutions drift because people drift."

"Mission fades the moment obedience becomes optional."

No institution begins corrupt.
Nations are not born wicked.
Churches do not drift instantly.
Families do not collapse overnight.
Movements do not abandon their mission in a moment.

Disorder enters institutions the way decay enters a building: slowly, quietly, invisibly at first — through small cracks, small compromises, small misalignments — until the structure no longer reflects the purpose for which it was created.

This is a biblical pattern:

- Eden was a perfect environment until disobedience entered.
- Israel was a covenant nation until idolatry corrupted the priesthood.
- The first-century church stood in power until false teachers infiltrated the flock.
- The temple intended for God's presence became a marketplace.

Institutions drift because people drift.

They inherit the fears, ambitions, deceptions, and desires of their leaders and participants. When people lose Divine Order, institutions do too.

Understanding **how** disorder enters an institution is essential to recognizing the patterns God is exposing in our time.

Institutions Drift When Mission Becomes Secondary

Every God-given institution has a purpose:

1. Marriage exists to display covenant love.
2. Family exists to form identity and nurture righteousness.
3. Civil authority exists to restrain evil and promote justice.
4. The church exists to make disciples and reveal Christ's kingdom.

When mission becomes secondary — even subtly — disorder begins.

This drift often starts small:

1. Shifting from obedience to outcomes
2. Elevating success over faithfulness
3. Prioritizing growth over holiness
4. Valuing comfort over conviction
5. Exchanging truth for popularity

Institutions collapse when they lose sight of why they exist.

Purpose is the spine of Divine Order.

Without purpose, the structure weakens.

Disorder Enters Through Misplaced Authority

Authority is a gift from God — but it is also a responsibility that must remain anchored in His character.

When authority is:

1. abused
2. neglected
3. distorted
4. centralized in the wrong hands
5. stripped away from its God-given boundaries

Michael A. Kovach
…then disorder floods in.

Scripture shows this repeatedly:

1. Eli refused to correct his sons, and corruption entered the priesthood.
2. Saul misused authority out of fear, and the kingdom fractured.
3. The Pharisees elevated tradition over Scripture, and worship was corrupted.

Authority is meant to protect, guide, nourish, and serve — not to control, manipulate, or dominate.

When authority becomes self-serving, institutions begin to mirror their leaders instead of their Lord.

Disorder Enters Through the Fear of Man

Fear is one of the most potent forces shaping institutional decisions.

Leaders who fear criticism make decisions for applause, not obedience. Boards that fear backlash remain silent when they should repent. Congregations that fear culture adapt doctrine to remain comfortable. Families that fear conflict avoid correction and accountability.

Fear produces:

1. Appeasement
2. Compromise
3. Silence
4. Indecision
5. Instability
6. Blurred boundaries

Fear of man is the doorway through which disorder walks into an institution.

This is why Scripture says:

"The fear of man brings a snare,
But whoever trusts in the Lord shall be safe."
—Proverbs 29:25 (NKJV)

Institutions built on fear collapse.
Institutions built on trust endure.

Disorder Enters Through Tolerated Sin

Sometimes disorder does not rush in — it drips in.

A small compromise is tolerated, so it grows.
A destructive pattern is excused, so it spreads.
A harmful relationship is ignored, so it gains influence.
A false teaching goes unchallenged, so it multiplies.

Sin spreads through institutions the way yeast spreads through dough.

Paul warned the Corinthian church:
"A little leaven leavens the whole lump." (1 Corinthians 5:6, NKJV)

Unchecked sin becomes institutional rot.

The danger is not just the sin itself —the danger is that people become accustomed to it.

What once grieved now feels normal.
What once shocked now feels acceptable.
What once offended now feels enlightened.

Tolerated sin reshapes the identity of an institution.

Disorder Enters When Truth Is Separated From Love

Truth without love becomes harsh and brittle.
Love without truth becomes permissive and blind.

Michael A. Kovach

Institutions fall into disorder through either extreme:

1. Legalism that crushes
2. Emotionalism that compromises
3. Dogmatism that divides
4. Sentimentality that erodes holiness

But Scripture holds the two in perfect tension:

"Speaking the truth in love… we are to grow up in all aspects into Him."
(Ephesians 4:15, NASB95)

Truth directs.
Love anchors.
Spirit empowers.

Remove any one of the three, and disorder infiltrates the structure.

Disorder Enters When Vision Replaces Revelation

Vision is a valuable tool — but it is not a substitute for revelation.

Human vision says, "Here is what we want to build."
Divine revelation says, "Here is what God is building."

Many churches, ministries, families, and organizations drift because they begin to rely on:

1. Strategic plans
2. Branding
3. Innovation
4. Systems
5. Marketing
6. Leadership models

These are not sinful.
But they become deadly substitutes when they displace God's presence and direction.

Moses refused to move without God's presence (Exodus 33:15).
Today, many institutions move faster than they listen.

Disorder grows wherever revelation is replaced by ambition.

The Inevitable Result: The Structure Reflects the Drift

When Divine Order is lost, institutions display predictable symptoms:

1. Confusion in direction
2. Inconsistency in leadership
3. Division among members
4. Mission drift
5. Moral compromise
6. Loss of spiritual authority
7. Increasing dependence on external validation
8. Declining spiritual vitality

Disorder produces institutions that look functional but lack life —like the fig tree Jesus cursed: leafy, impressive, and barren.

This is why Jesus warned that **every plant the Father has not planted will be uprooted** (Matthew 15:13).

Institutions grown from anything, but Divine Order cannot bear fruit.

The Hope: Institutions Can Be Restored

The good news is that institutional disorder is not final.
God restores institutions the same way He restores individuals:

1. Through repentance
2. Through truth
3. Through humility
4. Through courageous obedience
5. Through purified leadership
6. Through renewed mission

Michael A. Kovach
7.   Through the fear of God
8.   Through the work of the Spirit

When an institution — whether home, church, ministry, or nation — bows again to the authority of God, Divine Order returns.

Restoration is possible because the King reigns.

Conclusion:

Disorder enters institutions gradually, predictably, and invisibly — but it is not unstoppable.
It is the result of drift, compromise, fear, and misplaced authority.

But Divine Order brings:

1.   Clarity
2.   Strength
3.   Unity
4.   Stability
5.   Holiness
6.   Purpose
7.   Fruitfulness

Institutions reflect the hearts of the people within them.
When the people return to God, the institutions follow.

This is why Book 3 will now move into the next vital question:

What happens when believers inside those institutions drift into counterfeit Christianity?

CHAPTER FIVE

Discerning True Discipleship in an Age of Counterfeits

Discipleship is not admiration—it is allegiance."

"Selective obedience is disobedience wearing a religious mask."

Jesus' question to His disciples still echoes through history with uncompromising clarity:

"But who do you say that I am?"— Matthew 16:15 (NASB95)

This is not merely a theological question. It is a **dividing line**, a truth that separates genuine disciples from cultural followers.

Every believer, every generation, and every nation eventually reaches a moment when this question must be answered—not with emotion, not with tradition, not with borrowed conviction, but with **a surrendered life**.

In a world that increasingly embraces spiritual ambiguity, moral relativism, and religious pluralism, the question "Where do you stand?" has become essential. Not to shame, but to awaken. Not to condemn, but to clarify.

Because the greatest danger in the modern church is not atheism—it is **counterfeit Christianity**.

The Illusion of Discipleship

Many professing believers live with the assumption that they are disciples of Jesus simply because they:

1.   Attend church
2.   Pray occasionally
3.   Own a Bible

Michael A. Kovach
4.   Identify as Christian
5.   Avoid "major" sins
6.   Affirm Christian morals

But discipleship is not defined by **affiliation**; it is defined by **allegiance**.

A disciple is someone who:

1.   Follows Christ unconditionally
2.   Submits to His authority
3.   Embraces His teachings
4.   Rejects competing loyalty
5.   Lives in obedience regardless of cost

An unsubmitted believer is not a disciple. They are spectators.

The Danger of Selective Obedience

Selective obedience is the most common form of spiritual self-deception.

It sounds like:

1.   "I'll follow God in this area, but not in that one."
2.   "I believe Scripture, except the parts that challenge me."
3.   "I'll obey when it feels right."
4.   "I'll surrender when I'm ready."

But partial obedience is **disobedience in disguise**.

Jesus said:

"Why do you call Me, 'Lord, Lord,' and do not do what I say?" — Luke 6:46 (NASB95)

The modern church is filled with believers who claim Christ but reserve the right to overrule Him.

Where do you stand? Where Scripture confronts your comfort, **who wins?**

The Drift Into Cultural Christianity

Cultural Christianity is a faith shaped by society rather than by Scripture. It affirms Jesus socially but denies Him practically.

Signs of cultural Christianity include:

1. Faith is built on emotion rather than truth
2. Morality is shaped by popular opinion
3. Holiness dismissed as extremism
4. Doctrine avoided for fear of offense
5. Righteousness replaced by relevance
6. Repentance replaced with affirmation

True Discipleship Requires a Cost

Jesus never softened the cost of following Him.
He said:

"If anyone wishes to come after Me, he must deny himself, and take up his cross daily and follow Me." — Luke 9:23 (NASB95)

This cost includes:

1. Denying self-will
2. Rejecting sin
3. Surrendering pride
4. Forsaking worldly approval
5. Enduring persecution
6. Embracing holiness
7. Obeying without negotiation

The cross is not an accessory—it is a **death sentence** to the version of self that refuses Divine Order.

A disciple must choose between the comfort of culture and the cost of Christ. There is no middle ground.

Michael A. Kovach
The Illusion of Private Faith

Many Christians today have embraced the idea of a **private** faith—a faith that never speaks truth publicly, never confronts deception, never stands against cultural pressure.

But a faith that never costs anything is a faith that means nothing.

Jesus said:

"Whoever denies Me before men, I will also deny him before My Father who is in heaven." — Matthew 10:33 (NASB95)

Silence is not neutrality—it is agreement.

A disciple must speak truth even when culture demands silence.

The Need for Moral Courage

True discipleship requires moral courage—the willingness to stand for truth when truth is costly.

This courage is not personality-driven. It is Spirit-driven.

Courage appears when:

1. Convictions outweigh comfort
2. Holiness outweighs acceptance
3. Truth outweighs emotion
4. Obedience outweighs convenience
5. Christ outweighs everything

In an age of compromise, courage is the mark of a genuine disciple.

Where do you stand when standing costs you something?

The Evidence of a True Disciple

A disciple is known not by their words, but by their fruit:

1. Unwavering obedience
2. Love rooted in truth
3. Humility before God
4. Repentance when convicted
5. Endurance through trials
6. Rejection of hypocrisy
7. Increasing holiness
8. Courage in the face of pressure
9. Joy in surrender
10. Desire for God above self

If these marks are present, even imperfectly, discipleship is real.
If they are absent, even if religion is present, discipleship is counterfeit.

The Danger of Delay

Many believers assume they will "get serious" about their faith later—after retirement, after life settles down, after they feel ready.

But delay is one of the enemy's greatest weapons. It keeps believers imprisoned in good intentions that never become transformation.

There is no future version of you that will obey God if the present version refuses.

Discipleship is not a future decision—it is a present surrender.

Conclusion:

The question before every believer is the same today as it was 2,000 years ago:

Where do you stand?

Not where do you worship,
Not where do you attend,
Not where do you serve,
But **where do you stand** — in your heart,
In your obedience,

Michael A. Kovach
In your allegiance,
In your discipleship.

Christ does not ask for admiration.
He asks for surrender.

And in the days ahead, when truth becomes costly and compromise becomes easy, this question will define the difference between those who endure and those who fall away.

CHAPTER SIX

Why Many Believers Drift Into Counterfeit Christianity — The Quiet Seduction of Almost-Truth

---

"Counterfeit Christianity is the faith of almost—almost obedient, almost-surrendered, almost-holy."

"The flesh imitates spirituality to avoid surrender to the Spirit."

Counterfeit Christianity rarely begins in rebellion.
It begins in **almost obedience, almost holiness, almost surrender.**

It looks right.
Sounds right.
Feels right.
But lacks the substance and power of authentic faith.

Paul warned of those who have:

"…a form of godliness, although they have denied its power…"
— 2 Timothy 3:5 (NASB95)

Counterfeits imitate faith without experiencing transformation.

It is the faith that looks right, sounds right, feels right — but lacks the substance, authority, and power of genuine life in Christ.

Jesus warned that in the last days many would have **"a form of godliness but deny its power"** (2 Timothy 3:5, NASB95).
Not no godliness — form of godliness.
Not open rebellion — quiet substitution.
Not hostility — harmless imitation.

Counterfeit Christianity is not the opposite of faith;
it is the imitation of faith without the transformation of faith.

Michael A. Kovach

This chapter explores why so many drift into this condition — and why it is one of the greatest threats to the church in the modern age.

The Drift Begins With Misaligned Desires

Every believer experiences conflict between the inner man and the outer man. But drift begins when desires begin shifting away from obedience and toward comfort.

People do not wake up one day and decide to abandon discipleship. They drift because they begin wanting something God does not want for them:

1. Approval
2. Acceptance
3. Recognition
4. Ease
5. Predictability
6. Emotional security
7. The avoidance of conflict

When desire misaligns, obedience becomes inconvenient.
And when obedience becomes inconvenient, compromise becomes logical.

Desire always shapes direction.

The Drift Deepens When Truth Becomes Negotiable

Counterfeit Christianity thrives where truth is flexible.

Truth is not merely believed;
Truth must be submitted to.

But when believers begin:

1. Bending Scripture to fit personal preference
2. Ignoring passages that demand repentance
3. Reinterpreting holiness as legalism
4. Elevating feelings over revelation

5.   Following cultural narratives instead of biblical ones

…truth becomes negotiable.

Negotiable truth produces negotiable discipleship.

Once Scripture loses authority, everything becomes a matter of opinion.

The Drift Spreads When Community Reinforces It

People seldom drift alone.
They drift along with communities that normalize compromise.

Many believers surround themselves with:

1.   Communities that never correct
2.   Leaders who avoid confrontation
3.   Churches that celebrate sincerity over sanctification
4.   Friendships that value comfort over truth
5.   Teaching that soothes rather than sanctifies

A believer rarely rises above the spiritual honesty of the community they belong to.

A compromised community produces compromised Christians.

The Drift Accelerates When Conviction Is Silenced

The Spirit always warns before drift becomes deception.
Conviction is the sign of God's mercy — the alarm that says, *"Turn back now."*

But drift accelerates when conviction is:

1.   Ignored

Michael A. Kovach
2.	Delayed
3.	Rationalized
4.	Silenced
5.	Explained away
6.	Overridden by emotion

Conviction is not condemnation; it is rescue.
But when believers suppress conviction long enough, their spiritual senses dull.

The heart becomes calloused.
The conscience becomes numb.
Discernment becomes cloudy.

Once conviction is silenced, counterfeit Christianity feels normal.

The Drift Solidifies When Outward Faith Replaces Inward Life

Jesus confronted those who honored Him with their lips while their hearts were far from Him (Matthew 15:8). This describes the core of counterfeit Christianity:

Outward devotion without inward transformation.

People may:

1.	Attend church
2.	Pray publicly
3.	Serve in ministries
4.	Give generously
5.	Post Bible verses
6.	Speak Christian vocabulary

Yet avoid surrender, repentance, accountability, obedience, and holiness.

This is not discipleship — this is spiritual performance.

Christ does not merely want behavior; He wants allegiance.

The Drift Hardens When the Will Is Misunderstood

Many believers assume the Christian life is powered by human will —that sanctification is simply a matter of trying harder.

This misunderstanding leads to two outcomes:

Failure → Condemnation

Those who cannot sustain perfection believe they are unworthy.

Success → Pride

Those who manage superficial morality believe they are spiritual.

Both outcomes produce counterfeit Christianity.

The will was never designed to carry the Christian life.
The Spirit empowers what the will agrees with.
But pride convinces believers they can manage Christianity on their own terms.

That is the birthplace of religious counterfeits.

The Drift Becomes Dangerous When Pride Defends It

Once drift solidifies, pride begins to protect it.

Pride refuses:

1. Correction
2. Rebuke
3. Accountability
4. Scripture's authority
5. The Spirit's conviction

Michael A. Kovach

6.   The call to repentance

Pride can quote Scripture.
Pride can teach Scripture.
Pride can defend sin with Scripture.
Pride can justify compromise with theology.
Pride can disguise itself as confidence, wisdom, or enlightenment.

Pride does not destroy quickly — it destroys thoroughly.

This is why God resists the proud and gives grace to the humble (James 4:6, NKJV).

The Final Stage: Living Near Christ Without Living in Him

Perhaps the most sobering reality of counterfeit Christianity is this:

People can be near Jesus and never know Him.

Judas was near Him.
The Pharisees studied Him.
Crowds followed Him.
False prophets use His name.
Demons recognize His authority.

But only disciples *obey* Him.

Jesus' warning in Matthew 7:21-23 is not for atheists. It is for believers who mistake activity for intimacy:

"Many will say to Me... 'Did we not prophesy... cast out demons... perform miracles?' And then I will declare to them, 'I never knew you.'"

Counterfeit Christianity is not the absence of activity. It is the absence of a relationship.

Nearness without surrender is deception. Activity without obedience is rebellion dressed as religion.

The Way Home: Returning to Divine Order

The good news is that drift is not destiny.

Believers trapped in counterfeit Christianity can return — And the path back is the same path God always provides:

1.   **Truth:** Scripture above emotion
2.   **Repentance:** genuine turning, not simple regret
3.   **Surrender:** yielding the will to Christ
4.   **Obedience:** walking in holiness
5.   **Community:** accountability and correction
6.   **Spirit:** allowing Him to convict, teach, refine, and lead

Divine Order restores what has been distorted.

The goal is not shame — it is revival.
Not condemnation — restoration.
Not exposure — healing.

The Father does not reject drifting children; He calls them home.

Conclusion:

Counterfeit Christianity is not a fringe issue —it is one of the greatest dangers facing the modern church.

Because it:

1.   Looks holy
2.   Sounds holy
3.   Feels holy
4.   Yet resists the true life of holiness

But the Spirit is exposing this drift in our time so that:

1.   The church may awaken
2.   Believers may be purified
3.   Deception may be destroyed

Michael A. Kovach

4.　　　　Divine Order may be restored
5.　　　　The bride may be prepared

For the King is coming — and only surrendered disciples will recognize His voice when He calls.

CHAPTER SEVEN

The Cost of True Discipleship in the Last Days — Courage, Clarity, and Conviction

---

"The cross is not an accessory; it is the death of the self that refuses Divine Order."

"Obedience that costs nothing transforms nothing."

The greatest crisis facing the church is not external persecution—it is internal confusion about what it means to follow Christ.

Modern Christianity often seeks a comfortable Jesus.
A convenient Jesus.
A cultural Jesus.

But Jesus offered the cross, not comfort.

True discipleship is costly. But the reward is eternal.

Every generation of believers has faced challenges, but not every generation has faced a crisis of **definition**. Today, the most significant battle facing the church is not persecution from the world — it is confusion within the church about what it means to follow Christ.

Many want:

- Jesus' peace without His precepts
- Jesus' blessings without His boundaries
- Jesus' love without His lordship
- Jesus' comfort without His cross

But Jesus never offered an easy discipleship. He offered a costly one.

Michael A. Kovach

He said: "If anyone wishes to come after Me, he must deny himself, and take up his cross daily and follow Me." (Luke 9:23, NASB95)

Don't admire me.
Please do not believe in Me from a distance.
Do not associate with me casually.
Don't add me to your existing life.

Deny yourself.
Take up your cross.
Follow Me.

This is the discipleship Christ requires — and the discipleship many have forgotten.

Discipleship Has Always Been Costly

The first disciples left:

1. Homes
2. Livelihoods
3. Reputations
4. Social status
5. Safety
6. Comfort
7. Plans
8. Expectations

They followed Christ into uncertainty, danger, misunderstanding, and sacrifice — not because obedience was convenient, but because obedience was *right*.

In the first century, following Jesus meant:

1. Tension with families
2. Rejection from religious leaders
3. Suspicion from political authorities
4. Persecution from society
5. Mockery, imprisonment, and sometimes death

The cost was clear.
The choice was uncompromised.
The path was narrow.

The path has not changed.
Only our expectations have.

The Illusion of Casual Christianity

Modern culture has created a version of Christianity that requires no courage.

A Christianity where:

1.	Convenience replaces commitment
2.	Comfort replaces sacrifice
3.	Preference replaces obedience
4.	Inclusion replaces holiness
5.	Cultural acceptance replaces biblical conviction

This illusion is not discipleship — it is domesticated religion.

Discipleship calls us into the fire, but cultural Christianity calls us into comfort.

Jesus calls us into transformation, but cultural Christianity calls us into self-preservation.

The result is believers who want the crown but not the cross.

The Cost: Denying the Self

The first cost of discipleship is the most offensive in a self-centered age:

Self-denial.

Self:

Michael A. Kovach

1.   Demands to be pleased
2.   Demands to be affirmed
3.   Demands to be entertained
4.   Demands to be justified
5.   Demands to be protected
6.   Demands to be comforted

But Jesus says:

"Deny it."

Deny your ego.
Deny your preferences.
Deny your habits.
Deny your fantasies of control.
Deny your flesh's demands.
Deny your desire to be your own master.

Self-denial is not self-hatred — it is surrender to the rightful King.

The Cost: Taking Up the Cross

In the first century, the cross was not a symbol of religion — it was a symbol of death.

To take up your cross meant:

1.   You were under sentence
2.   You had no future of your own
3.   You had no claim on your own life
4.   You had surrendered control
5.   You were walking toward obedience, even if it cost everything

Taking up your cross means embracing the death of:

1.   Pride
2.   Stubbornness
3.   Rebellion
4.   Ambition
5.   Autonomy
6.   The illusion of control

We cannot walk in Divine Order while dragging the carcass of self-rule behind us.

The cross is not an accessory.
It is the doorway into life.

The Cost: Following Jesus, Not the World

Jesus said, "**Follow Me.**"
Not culture.
Not comfort.
Not the majority opinion.
Not appetites.
Not politics.
Not trends.
Not emotions.

Following Christ requires:

1.   Courage to be misunderstood
2.   Courage to be disliked
3.   Courage to stand alone
4.   Courage to speak the truth
5.   Courage to resist the world's pressure
6.   courage to obey when obedience is costly

Cowardice produces compromise.
Courage produces disciples.

The Cost: Obedience Without Negotiation

We live in a time when believers negotiate with God:

1.   "I'll obey if I agree."
2.   "I'll follow if it feels right."
3.   "I'll surrender if it doesn't cost too much."
4.   "I'll serve if I have time."

But negotiated obedience is disobedience in disguise.

Michael A. Kovach
Discipleship means:

1. Obeying when we don't understand
2. Obeying when we don't feel like it
3. Obeying when it costs us something
4. Obeying when obedience divides us from culture
5. Obeying even when following Christ isolates us

Obedience is not convenient — it is costly. But obedience is where Divine Order begins.

The Cost: Standing Firm in the Last Days

Paul warned that "all who desire to live godly in Christ Jesus will be persecuted" (2 Timothy 3:12, NASB95).

Not might be. **Will be.**

In the last days, the cost of discipleship will intensify:

1. Hostility toward truth
2. Pressure to compromise holiness
3. Redefining sin as virtue
4. Persecution for biblical convictions
5. Cultural marginalization
6. Relational loss
7. Economic consequences
8. Spiritual warfare

The last days will separate admirers of Jesus from servants of Jesus.

The only believers who will endure are those who choose conviction over comfort.

The Reward: A Life Aligned With the King

The cost of discipleship is high, but the reward is immeasurable:

1. Intimacy with Christ
2. Clarity of purpose

3.	Power of the Spirit
4.	Freedom from the flesh
5.	Boldness in truth
6.	Endurance in trials
7.	Transformation into Christ's image
8.	Preparation for the kingdom to come

The cross is costly, but it leads to resurrection.

Obedience is costly, but it leads to transformation.

Holiness is costly, but it leads to joy.

Discipleship is costly, but it leads to life.

Conclusion:

True discipleship is not for the faint of heart — it is for the surrendered heart.

Counterfeit Christianity costs nothing and produces nothing. True discipleship costs everything and produces eternal fruit.

In these last days, the Spirit is raising up believers who will stand with courage, clarity, and conviction — not because they are strong, but because they are aligned with the One who is.

The King is coming.
And His disciples must be ready.

Being ready means walking in the divine order He restored—living as those guided by His Spirit, aligned with His truth, and rooted in His Kingdom. Readiness is not passive waiting; it's active engagement in His mission of reconciliation. It's the quiet courage of obedience, the consistent practice of love, and the daily decision to let His life transform ours.

The return of the King reveals not only His glory but also the fulfillment of everything He began in us. Let us, then, live as people of the coming age even while we walk in this one.

Michael A. Kovach

He has not called us to fear His return, but to be ready and prepared to welcome Him.

CHAPTER EIGHT

The Great Misunderstanding — The Will, the Flesh, and the Spirit's Work in Us

---

"The will can agree with God, but only the Spirit can accomplish what God commands."

> "The flesh doesn't resist God by rebellion alone—it resists Him through imitation."

One of the most persistent misunderstandings in the Christian life is the confusion surrounding **the human will after salvation**. Many believers assume that once they come to Christ, their will becomes automatically righteous, automatically aligned, and automatically capable of producing holiness.

But Scripture teaches something different.
Something deeper.
Something far more humbling — and far more hopeful.

The tension between **will, flesh,** and **Spirit** is not a flaw in the Christian life; it is a design God uses to transform us. But when this tension is misunderstood, believers fall into cycles of guilt, striving, frustration, and discouragement. Some assume they are failing God. Others assume God is failing them.

The truth is this:
The will can agree with God, but it cannot accomplish holiness. Only the Spirit can.

This chapter exposes the misunderstanding that has shaped much of modern discipleship and shows how Divine Order brings clarity, peace, and freedom.

Michael A. Kovach

The Will Is Not the Power Source of the Christian Life

People often say:

1. "I need to try harder."
2. "I need more self-control."
3. "I just have to force myself to be better."
4. "I need more discipline."

But Scripture never says the will transforms us.

Paul writes:

"For I know that nothing good dwells in me, that is, in my flesh; for the willing is present in me, but the doing of the good is not."
— Romans 7:18 (NASB95)

The will can **desire** what is right, but it cannot **produce** what is right.

This is the great misunderstanding.

The will was never designed to power the Christian life. It was intended to **agree** with the Spirit, not to **replace** the Spirit.

The Flesh Is the Pretender

The flesh is not merely sin; it is the entire system of self-rule inherited from Adam.

The flesh says:

1. "I can do this."
2. "I don't need help."
3. "I'm strong enough."
4. "I can obey on my own."
5. "I just need more willpower."

But the flesh is a liar. It imitates strength to avoid surrender.

Paul describes the flesh as hostile to God:

"The mind set on the flesh is hostile toward God; for it does not subject itself to the law of God, for it is not even able to do so." — Romans 8:7 (NASB95)

The flesh does not obey God because it **cannot** obey God.

This is why the Christian life becomes exhausting when the flesh tries to imitate obedience.

Clarifying "In Jesus' Name"

When Jesus taught His disciples to pray, He did not instruct them to address prayer to Himself, nor did He offer a formula meant to compel divine action. He taught them to pray, *"Our Father who is in heaven."* In doing so, Jesus established both the direction and the order of prayer.

To pray *in Jesus' name* is not to recite a verbal credential, nor is it an incantation appended to a request. In Scripture, a name represents authority, alignment, and commission. To pray in Jesus' name is to pray in alignment with His character, His teaching, and His will—approaching the Father on the basis of Christ's mediation, not personal desire.

Vague prayers addressed simply to "God," without regard for who that God is, reflect a loss of discernment. Scripture does not treat "god" as a neutral category. Jesus reveals the Father, and prayer that ignores that revelation risks becoming directionless, self-referential, or manipulative.

Biblical prayer flows upward—from the believer, through Christ, by the Spirit, to the Father in heaven. Any prayer that reverses this order subtly bends communion back toward the self, undermining the very relationship prayer is meant to cultivate.

Michael A. Kovach

The Spirit Does What the Will Cannot

The Spirit does not merely influence the Christian life—He **empowers** it.

He:

1.   Convicts
2.   Guides
3.   Strengthens
4.   Purifies
5.   Aligns
6.   Empowers obedience
7.   Produces fruit
8.   Reveals truth
9.   Breaks patterns
10.   Transforms the inner man

Paul teaches:

"Walk by the Spirit, and you will not carry out the desire of the flesh."
— Galatians 5:16 (NASB95)

This is not a suggestion; it is an explanation.

We resist the flesh not by willpower, but by **yielding** to the Spirit.

Why So Many Believers Feel Like Failures

Because they assume:

1.   Holiness comes from personal effort
2.   Transformation comes from trying harder
3.   Obedience comes from determination
4.   Victory comes from self-discipline

And when they inevitably fail, they think:

1.   "Maybe I'm not saved."
2.   "Maybe I'm too weak."
3.   "Maybe God is disappointed."

4.   "Maybe I'm broken beyond repair."

No — they are simply trying to live the Christian life in a way God never intended.

The will is **not** the engine. The Spirit is.

The will is the **steering wheel**. The Spirit is the **power train**.

Confusing these roles produces discouragement and exhaustion.

The Flesh Loves Religious Activity

One of the most dangerous patterns in the Christian life is when the flesh discovers it can be religious.

The flesh will:

1.   Attend church
2.   Serve in ministry
3.   Study Scripture
4.   Pray publicly
5.   Behave morally

— all while refusing to surrender.

The flesh imitates spiritual life without experiencing transformation.

This is why Jesus said:

"These people honor Me with their lips, But their heart is far away from Me." — Matthew 15:8 (NASB95)

The flesh can perform. Only the Spirit can transform.

The Battle Between Will and Flesh

Paul captures this battle perfectly:

Michael A. Kovach

"For the good that I want, I do not do, but I practice the very evil that I do not want." — Romans 7:19 (NASB95)

This is not the cry of an unbeliever — this is the voice of a man who understands the spiritual conflict inside every believer.

The will **wants** what God wants.
The flesh refuses to cooperate.
And the Spirit works to bring both into Divine Order.

This conflict is not proof of spiritual failure; it is proof of spiritual life.

Dead people do not wrestle.
Only the living do.

Transformation Happens Through Surrender, Not Striving

The key to spiritual growth is not willpower; it is surrender.

Jesus didn't say:

1. "Try harder."
2. "Push through."
3. "Discipline yourself more."

He said:

"Abide in Me." — John 15:4 (NASB95)

Abiding is not striving.
Abiding is yielding.

Holiness is not the result of human effort; it is the fruit of divine presence.
The Spirit transforms what the will cannot touch.

Freedom Comes From Alignment

Freedom is not the absence of struggle.
Freedom is the presence of alignment.

When:

1.	The will agrees with the Spirit
2.	The mind is renewed by truth
3.	The flesh is denied its authority
4.	The heart is surrendered
5.	The Spirit empowers obedience

… Divine Order forms inside the believer.

This is the life Jesus promised:
Not easy, but empowered.
Not perfect, but aligned.
Not effortless, but Spirit-led.

Conclusion:

The great misunderstanding of the Christian life is the belief that the will can produce what only the Spirit can accomplish.

The will has value.
It can agree with God.
It can choose to surrender.
It can humble itself.
It can say "yes" to truth.

But it cannot transform the heart.

That is the Spirit's work.

Understanding this frees the believer from guilt, striving, and exhaustion. It brings clarity, peace, and alignment with Divine Order. It prepares the way for Chapter 9, where we expose how the flesh disguises itself as strength — and how the Spirit reveals the truth behind those disguises.

Michael A. Kovach

CHAPTER NINE

How the Flesh Masquerades as Strength — And How the Spirit Breaks the Illusion

---

"False strength resists surrender; true strength is born from it."

"The flesh hides behind competence, so it never has to bow."

The greatest threat to spiritual maturity is not always sin in its obvious forms — it is the **flesh pretending to be strength**. What most believers interpret as willpower, determination, confidence, conviction, stability, or resilience is often nothing more than the flesh in disguise.

And the flesh loves disguise.

It rarely announces itself as rebellion.
It rarely appears as stubbornness.
It rarely reveals its motives honestly.

Instead, the flesh often dresses itself in the language of:

1. Discernment
2. Wisdom
3. Maturity
4. Boldness
5. Zeal
6. Caution
7. Conviction

When the flesh wants to take control, it simply borrows spiritual vocabulary. This is why the believer must learn to distinguish **true spiritual strength** from the flesh's imitation. The two feel similar, but their fruits are radically different.

The Flesh Imitates Strength Through Stubbornness

Many believers confuse **stubbornness** with **strength of will**, but stubbornness is not strength — it is resistance to Divine Order.

Stubbornness says:

1. "I know what's best."
2. "I can handle this."
3. "I don't need correction."
4. "I don't need help."
5. "I'm right, no matter what Scripture or counsel says."

Stubbornness feels like confidence, but it is self-protection.

Oswald Chambers captured this truth:
"Your will agrees with God; it is your stubbornness that refuses."

Stubbornness disguises itself as spiritual resilience, but it is the flesh clinging to control.

True strength yields.
False strength resists.

The Flesh Imitates Strength Through Self-Reliance

The flesh loves to whisper:

"You're strong enough.
You're disciplined enough.
You're smart enough.
You're spiritual enough."

Self-reliance is the flesh's attempt to live the Christian life **without the Spirit**.

Michael A. Kovach

It produces:

1. Exhaustion
2. Frustration
3. Burnout
4. Discouragement
5. Pride when successful
6. Shame when failing

When believers rely on themselves, they are relying on the very thing Christ came to crucify.

Self-reliance feels strong, but it is a spiritual weakness masquerading as strength.

The Flesh Imitates Strength Through Pride

Pride is the flesh's armor.

It protects the ego.
It avoids vulnerability.
It refuses accountability.
It hides insecurity behind confidence.
It hides brokenness behind competence.
It hides rebellion behind self-righteousness.

Pride can preach sermons.
Pride can lead ministries.
Pride can serve faithfully.
Pride can teach truth.
Pride can look holy.

But pride cannot obey.

Pride resists surrender — and therefore resists Divine Order.

The Flesh Imitates Strength Through Emotional Control

Some believers mistake emotional suppression for spiritual strength. They assume that:

1.   Not crying
2.   Not confessing
3.   Not asking for help
4.   Not expressing weakness
5.   Not acknowledging pain

…is maturity.

But emotional suppression is not maturity — it is self-protection. It keeps the believer from being healed, corrected, or transformed.

The Spirit does not need emotional toughness. The Spirit needs an open heart.

The flesh hardens; The Spirit softens.

The Flesh Imitates Strength Through False Humility

False humility is one of the flesh's most deceptive disguises.

It sounds like:

1.   "I'm nothing."
2.   "I'm not worthy."
3.   "I can't do anything right."
4.   "God can't use someone like me."
5.   "I'm just a sinner saved by grace — nothing more."

This sounds spiritual, but it is pride inverted.

Michael A. Kovach

It is the flesh drawing attention to itself through self-deprecation.

False humility avoids responsibility, avoids calling, and avoids obedience.

True humility agrees with God's assessment:
Who He is, who we are, and who we are becoming in Christ.

False humility masks fear. True humility produces obedience.

The Flesh Imitates Strength Through Selective Obedience

Selective obedience is one of the most evident signs of the flesh.

The believer obeys where obedience is comfortable — but negotiates where obedience is costly.

The flesh loves:

1.   easy obedience
2.   partial obedience
3.   delayed obedience
4.   conditional obedience

But genuine obedience is costly. It requires surrender in every area, not just the safe ones.

Selective obedience feels strong — because the flesh gets to stay in control.

The Flesh Imitates Strength Through Hyper-Spirituality

Hyper-spirituality is the flesh wearing a religious costume.

It speaks in deep spiritual language.
It appears discerning.
It feels intense.
It loves dramatic expressions.
It claims spiritual insight while resisting correction.

Hyper-spirituality is the flesh pretending to be the Spirit.

It produces:

1.   Emotional intensity without stability
2.   Noise without holiness
3.   Activity without transformation
4.   Revelation without accountability

The Spirit produces fruit, not theatrics.

The Flesh Imitates Strength Through Moralism

Moralism is the flesh trying to be holy without the Spirit.

It focuses on:

1.   Behavior management
2.   Rule-keeping
3.   Image maintenance
4.   Avoiding "big sins."
5.   Producing an outward appearance of order

But moralism lacks:

1.   Transformation
2.   Love
3.   Joy
4.   Surrender
5.   Intimacy with God
6.   Spiritual power

Moralism is the flesh pretending to be sanctified.

Only the Spirit sanctifies.

Michael A. Kovach

How to Discern the Difference Between Flesh and Spirit

The flesh produces:

1. Defensiveness
2. Pride
3. Stubbornness
4. Hypocrisy
5. Anxiety
6. Comparison
7. Fear
8. Insecurity
9. Self-focus

The Spirit produces:

1. Humility
2. Peace
3. Conviction
4. Surrender
5. Fruitfulness
6. Stability
7. Wisdom
8. Love

The flesh always defends itself.
The Spirit always points to Christ.

The flesh fights for control.
The Spirit invites surrender.

The flesh seeks recognition.
The Spirit seeks obedience.

When believers learn this difference, they begin to see the flesh's disguises clearly — and Divine Order starts to take root.

Freedom Comes From Exposing the Flesh

The flesh has power only when hidden.

When exposed:

1.   Its lies lose influence
2.   Its disguises lose appeal
3.   Its strength collapses
4.   Its stubbornness weakens

The Spirit reveals the flesh not to shame us but to free us.

Transformation begins when believers finally admit:

"This is not strength — this is flesh pretending to be strong."

Once exposed, the Spirit begins to replace false strength with true strength:

1.   Strength rooted in surrender
2.   Strength rooted in obedience
3.   Strength rooted in holiness
4.   Strength rooted in truth
5.   Strength rooted in Divine Order
6.   Strength rooted in Christ Himself

This is the strength that endures.

Conclusion:

The flesh is a master of disguise. It imitates spiritual strength to keep control. But once the believer sees its patterns, its strategies, and its counterfeit forms of "strength," the deception collapses.

And when the flesh is unmasked, the believer finally becomes free to walk in:

1.   Humility
2.   Obedience

Michael A. Kovach

3. Purity
4. Clarity
5. Confidence
6. Courage
7. Spirit-led transformation

This is why Chapter 8 was foundational — and why the next chapter (Chapter 10) will reveal **how the Spirit exposes our blind spots** to restore Divine Order.

CHAPTER TEN

The Spirit's Work in Revealing Our Blind Spots — How God Illuminates What We Cannot See

---

"The Spirit reveals what we cannot see so He can heal what we cannot reach."

"Revelation is not condemnation—it is mercy."

One of the most gracious works of the Holy Spirit is His ability to reveal the things we cannot see about ourselves. Blind spots are the places where our flesh hides, our wounds distort perception, our pride defends itself, and our assumptions feel like truth.

Blind spots are not visible to us — they are visible **only** to the Spirit.

This is why Jesus said the Spirit would *"guide you into all the truth"* (John 16:13, NASB95).

Guiding into truth is not merely intellectual; it is transformational.
Truth exposes.
Truth illuminates.
Truth restores.

Every believer has blind spots.
Every church has blind spots.
Every generation has blind spots.

And the Spirit reveals them not to condemn, but to heal.

What Blind Spots Actually Are

Blind spots are areas where:

Michael A. Kovach

1.   We think we are strong, but we are weak
2.   We think we are right, but we are misaligned
3.   We think we are discerning, but we are deceived
4.   We think we are obedient, but we are selective
5.   We think we are humble, but we are proud
6.   We think we see clearly, but we see through wounds

Blind spots are spiritual distortions created by:

1.   Pride
2.   Fear
3.   Emotional wounds
4.   Unexamined habits
5.   Cultural influence
6.   Old patterns of thinking
7.   The flesh masquerading as strength (Chapter 9)

They form slowly, invisibly, and quietly — and only the Spirit can expose them.

Why the Spirit Reveals Blind Spots

The Spirit reveals blind spots for one central reason:

Because Divine Order cannot be restored where deception remains hidden.

Blind spots hinder:

1.   Obedience
2.   Discernment
3.   Intimacy with God
4.   Relational health
5.   Spiritual authority
6.   Purpose
7.   Transformation

God is too committed to His people to let them walk blindly.

He exposes what we hide.
He illuminates what we ignore.

He reveals what we misunderstand.
He confronts what we excuse.
He heals what we fear.

This exposure is grace, not judgment.

How the Spirit Reveals Blind Spots

The Spirit uses multiple tools to uncover what we cannot see:

1. Scripture

The Word of God is a mirror (James 1:23-24).
It exposes motives, patterns, sins, and desires that are invisible to us.

2. Conviction

Conviction is not guilt — it is clarity.
It is the Spirit's voice saying, *"Look here. This needs attention."*

3. Godly Counsel

Sometimes God reveals our blind spots through believers who love us
enough to speak truth, even when it is uncomfortable.

4. Trials

Pressure reveals the cracks we didn't know existed. Trials expose where we
trust ourselves more than God.

5. Delayed Answers

Sometimes God does not give us what we want until He shows us why we
want it.

6. Unanswered Prayer

Not because He is silent — but because He is exposing motives.

7. Repetition

Patterns that keep resurfacing often point to a blind spot we haven't confronted.

8. The Fruit Test

The Spirit examines not what we *intend*, but what our life produces.

When the Spirit reveals a blind spot, He does so with precision.
Not to shame — but to restore.

Why Blind Spots Are Difficult to Accept

When the Spirit exposes something, we cannot see, our first reaction is often resistance:

1.   "That's not me."
2.   "I'm not like that."
3.   "I didn't mean it that way."
4.   "People misunderstand me."
5.   "I have good intentions."

But intentions are not transformation.

Blind spots trigger defensiveness because they confront:

1.   Ego
2.   Control
3.   Identity
4.   Pride
5.   Comfort
6.   Self-protection

This is why growth requires humility.
We cannot be healed of what we insist does not exist.

Humility says:

"Lord, show me whatever I cannot see."

This is the posture of discipleship.

Biblical Examples of Blind Spot Revelation

Scripture is full of people who thought they were right — and God showed them otherwise:

David

He dismissed his sin with Bathsheba until Nathan confronted him.
A king with a blind spot.

Peter

Boldly insisted he would never deny Christ — then denied Him three times.
A disciple with a blind spot.

Jonah

Obeyed outwardly but resisted inwardly.
A prophet with a blind spot.

Martha

Served with sincerity yet missed the presence of Jesus. A servant with a blind spot.

The Pharisees

Knew Scripture but missed the Messiah standing before them.
A religious system with a blind spot.

Blind spots are not signs of weakness — they are signs of humanity.
And God reveals them because He loves us too much to leave us blind.

Michael A. Kovach

How the Flesh Fights the Spirit's Revelation

The flesh resists exposure because exposure threatens control.
When the Spirit reveals blind spots, the flesh responds with:

1. Defensiveness
2. Argument
3. Distraction
4. Justification
5. Withdrawal
6. Blame
7. Delay

The flesh hates light.
The Spirit is light.

This collision is the battle between Chapter 9's "masquerading strength" and the genuine work of the Spirit.

The flesh can imitate strength.
But it cannot imitate surrender.

What Happens When Blind Spots Are Revealed

When the Spirit uncovers a blind spot, and we yield to His work:

1. Clarity replaces confusion
2. Peace replaces inner tension
3. Humility replaces pride
4. Obedience becomes easier
5. Relationships heal
6. The purpose becomes clearer
7. Distractions lose their power
8. Stubbornness weakens
9. Intimacy with God deepens

Revelation is always followed by restoration.

This is why the Spirit exposes: **So that He may heal.**

What Happens When Blind Spots Are Ignored

If we resist revelation:

1.   Deception strengthens
2.   The flesh gains influence
3.   Patterns worsen
4.   Relationships fracture
5.   Spiritual growth stalls
6.   Conviction dulls
7.   Discernment fades
8.   Obedience becomes burdensome
9.   Disorder deepens

Blind spots ignored become strongholds.

Blind spots confronted become breakthroughs.

The Greatest Blind Spot: Believing We Have None

The most dangerous believer is not the one with a blind spot — it is the one who believes they have none.

A humble believer grows.
A teachable believer matures.
A yielded believer is transformed.

But a believer who cannot be corrected is a believer who cannot be restored.

This is why Jesus repeatedly said,
"He who has ears to hear, let him hear."

Not everyone has ears — but anyone can ask God for them.

Conclusion: Revelation Prepares Us for Restoration

Michael A. Kovach

Chapter 10 is the gateway to Chapter 12 — because recognizing blind spots is essential for recognizing patterns.

The Spirit reveals individual blind spots so the believer can then see the larger patterns of disorder in their heart, their relationships, their church, and their world.

This is how Divine Order begins: with light shining on the places, we could not see and truth guiding us where we could not go.

The next chapter (Chapter 11) will explore the personal journey God took you through — how these revelations unfolded across decades and prepared the ground for the full unveiling of Divine Order in Chapter 12.

CHAPTER ELEVEN

A Life Shaped Across Decades — How God Formed the Pattern Before the Language Existed

---

"What felt random in the moment becomes revelation in hindsight."

"God prepares the vessel long before He reveals the assignment."

This is the chapter that ties the personal story to the book's theological foundation. For years, I sensed patterns without understanding them. I saw drift in culture, compromise in the church, and conflict in the believer long before I understood their connection. At the time, I thought these were separate themes. Now I see that they were fragments of a larger revelation the Spirit was stitching together.

Divine Order was not a single insight. It was a lifetime of revelations converging into one truth.

The Early Years: Learning to Listen

In my early walk with Christ, I learned the value of listening. Not to noise, not to opinion, not even to tradition — but to the still, small voice of God. My hunger for Scripture was not academic; it was relational. I read to know Him. I studied to understand His heart. I prayed not merely to request, but to discern.

In those years, God taught me:

1. The difference between information and revelation
2. The danger of assuming maturity before it forms
3. The value of simple obedience
4. The importance of humility
5. The necessity of remaining teachable

Michael A. Kovach

The foundation was being laid, even if I didn't recognize the blueprint yet.

The Middle Years: Seeing Disorder Without Language

There came a time when I began to sense that something was deeply wrong in the world — not just morally or socially, but spiritually. I saw:

1.　　The drift of culture into fear (later captured in Chapter 2)
2.　　The collapse of discernment (Chapter 3)
3.　　The compromise in institutions (Chapter 4)

At the time, these observations felt like burdens. They were heavy, persistent, and deeply unsettling. But I lacked the theological framework to connect them.

God was showing me disorder — so that I would one day understand Divine Order.

Sometimes God reveals what is broken before He reveals what restores.

The Burden for the Church: A Call to Wakefulness

I carried for years a deep burden for the church — not for its structures, but for its people.

I saw believers drifting into:

1.　　Surface-level faith
2.　　Selective obedience
3.　　Emotional spirituality
4.　　Borrowed conviction
5.　　Counterfeit Christianity (Chapters 5 and 6)
6.　　Discipleship without surrender (Chapter 7)

I felt grief, not anger, concern, not condemnation. I saw what many refused to see — not because I was superior, but because the Spirit was revealing the early signs of collapse. At the time, I didn't understand why I saw these patterns so clearly. Now I know: God was preparing me to speak into them.

The Inner Journey: Wrestling With the Flesh

My own struggles became part of God's formation.

I learned the difference between:

1. will and stubbornness
2. strength and self-reliance
3. holiness and moralism
4. spiritual zeal and fleshly intensity
5. obedience and religious activity

I discovered firsthand how the flesh disguises itself (Chapter 9), how the believer misinterprets its influence (Chapter 8), and how the Spirit must reveal blind spots (Chapter 10).

These were not academic lessons — they were personal confrontations.

God was shaping me through:

1. failure and restoration
2. questions and answers
3. trials and breakthroughs
4. weakness and grace

The Spirit was not simply teaching me doctrine; He was building discernment in me.

The Long Arc: Revelation Through Time

Revelation does not always come in epiphanies — sometimes it comes in accumulation.

God speaks over the years.
He teaches over seasons.
He forms over decades.

Michael A. Kovach

And only when enough pieces are in place does the picture emerge.

That picture, for me, was this:

**Divine Order is the pattern behind everything God does —
and the absence of Divine Order is the pattern behind everything that
collapses.**

Cultural disorder.
Church disorder.
Personal disorder.
All different expressions of the same root problem.

This realization was the hinge that turned fragments into revelation.

The Turning Point: Recognizing God's Pattern

There came a moment — a quiet, unexpected moment — when the Spirit
connected everything:

1.   What I had seen in the culture
2.   What I had discerned in the church
3.   What I had wrestled with in my own heart

It was not a new revelation.
It was the illumination of what God had been teaching me all along.

I realized:

1.   Fear disrupts order
2.   Compromise destroys order
3.   Deception blinds order
4.   Pride resists order
5.   Sin fractures order
6.   Flesh imitates order
7.   Spirit restores order

These were not isolated insights. They were the anatomy of Divine Order.

For the first time, I saw the whole story — the story God had been writing
through my life.

The Assignment: Teaching Others to See

Once the revelation became clear, so did the assignment:

Help the church see what God has shown me.
Help believers discern the patterns.
Help the body understand Divine Order.
Help the Bride prepare for the return of the King.

This calling did not arise from ambition — it arose from responsibility.

God entrusted me with a message He had been forming in me for decades. It was not mine to keep; it was mine to steward.

Book 3 is the culmination of that stewardship.

Why This Chapter Matters

This chapter is personal — but it is also pastoral.

It shows the reader that revelation takes time.
That God teaches across seasons.
That clarity comes through obedience, humility, and surrender.
That the Spirit is patient, intentional, and consistent.

And it prepares the reader for Chapter 12, where the patterns are finally shown in full.

Chapter 11 is the testimony.
Chapter 12 is the revelation.

This chapter shows **how** God shaped the message.
The next chapter shows **what** the message means.

Conclusion:

God rarely reveals everything at once. He reveals enough for the next step — and forms us through obedience, one step at a time.

Michael A. Kovach

Looking back, I see the purpose in every burden, every insight, every confusion, every breakthrough.

God was not only teaching me —He was preparing me.

Preparing me to write these books.
Preparing me to see the patterns.
Preparing me to help others see them.
Preparing me for the message of Divine Order.

This is why Book 3 exists, not as a commentary on culture, but as a testimony to God's slow, faithful, patient revelation.

And now, with that story told, we turn to the revelation itself; Patterns Repeated — the chapter that brings it all together.

CHAPTER TWELVE

Recognizing the Pattern — How Divine Order Reveals What Disorder Tries to Hide

---

"Disorder is never random—it follows the same pattern across generations."

"Clarity begins when the Spirit trains the believer to see spiritually, not just logically."

When I look back over the decades of my life—through the sermons I heard, the Scriptures I studied, the burdens I carried, and the essays I wrote—I can now see a pattern that was not obvious at the time. It was buried beneath daily life, ministry assignments, personal trials, and hundreds of quiet moments with God.

But the pattern was always there. **God was showing me something long before I understood what I was seeing.**

This chapter is the hinge of Book 3.
It connects the decades of revelation with the clarity of Divine Order.
It shows why the Spirit highlighted cultural decline, institutional drift, church disorder, and inner tension.
And it explains the "thread" that binds all three books together.

Divine Order is not a doctrine.
It is a pattern woven into creation, into Scripture, into spiritual life, and into history itself.

And this chapter reveals how that pattern appeared repeatedly—until it finally came into focus.

Michael A. Kovach

The Early Fragments: Revelation Without Context

In my younger years, I received insights that felt important but incomplete.

I saw:

1.   Fear is spreading like a quiet disease through society
2.   Compromise creeping into churches
3.   Believers wrestling with inner division
4.   Institutions drifting from their mission
5.   Spiritual apathy replacing conviction
6.   Moral confusion is rising unexpectedly
7.   Scripture is being reinterpreted rather than obeyed.

But I did not yet know how these observations connected.

At the time, they felt like burdens—heavy but isolated.

Now I know: **These were early fragments of a larger revelation.**

God often reveals the pieces long before He reveals the picture.

The Middle Years: Seeing the Same Pattern in Different Places

As time moved on, something remarkable happened:

I began to see **the same pattern** repeating in completely different contexts.

In culture.
In churches.
In families.
In individual believers.
In myself.

The symptoms were different, but the underlying issue was the same:

Disorder follows the same path, no matter where it appears.

I could not yet articulate the pattern, but I could feel it.
Something was out of alignment.
Something foundational was missing.

Across decades, the Spirit kept highlighting these same movements:

1. confusion → compromise → collapse
2. fear → drift → deception
3. pride → blindness → destruction

It was like hearing the same melody playing faintly beneath every situation.

And slowly, the pattern became undeniable.

The Spirit's Consistency—Revelation Over Time

God does not rush revelation. He forms it.

He teaches gradually, layer by layer, through:

1. Scripture
2. Relationships
3. Trials
4. Failures
5. Questions
6. Assignments
7. Seasons of clarity
8. Seasons of silence
9. Years of reflection

And over time, the fragments begin to align. One day, you awaken to the realization:

"God has been teaching me the same thing all along."

Not because He repeats himself, but because we need repetition for understanding. The Spirit's consistency is not monotony — it is mercy.

Michael A. Kovach
The Pattern of Disorder

Through the years, I noticed that disorder always follows a predictable sequence:

1. Loss of Discernment

People stop distinguishing truth from error.

2. Loss of Holiness

Sin becomes normalized and even celebrated.

3. Loss of Identity

People forget who they are and why God created them.

4. Loss of Covenant

Relationships weaken, families fracture, and communities lose coherence.

5. Loss of Truth

Scripture is reinterpreted to fit preference.

6. Loss of Spiritual Authority

Churches weaken as compromise spreads.

7. Collapse

Chaos emerges where Divine Order is absent.

Whether in a person, a church, a community, or a nation, **the pattern is the same.**

This was the revelation forming inside me long before I had language for it.

The Pattern of Restoration

What amazed me even more was seeing the inverse pattern, God's pattern of **restoration**:

1. Revelation

God exposes what is broken.

2. Conviction

The Spirit awakens the heart.

3. Repentance

The will yields to God.

4. Purification

The flesh loses its authority.

5. Alignment

The believer returns to Divine Order.

6. Empowerment

The Spirit restores clarity, strength, and purpose.

7. Fruitfulness

Life, holiness, and stability return.

This pattern mirrors the journey of Israel, the early church, and every believer who has walked with God across time.

Michael A. Kovach
Disorder has a pattern.
Restoration has a pattern.
Both are ancient, predictable, and revealed in Scripture.

The Missing Piece Finally Appears

It took decades for the complete revelation to crystallize, but when it did, everything made sense.

The Spirit was not showing me isolated warnings. He was showing me a **single truth with many expressions:**

Where Divine Order is abandoned, disorder multiplies.
Where Divine Order is restored, life flourishes.

Book 1 explained the architecture of Divine Order.
Book 2 explained the relational consequences of disorder.
Book 3 reveals the patterns behind both—and why they matter now.

This was the moment the threads came together.
This is when I finally understood what the Spirit had been showing me for years.

Why This Matters Now

We are living in a time of increasing instability, morally, culturally, spiritually, and relationally.

The patterns are repeating.
The drift is accelerating.
The signs are unmistakable.

But so is the hope.

God reveals the pattern of disorder **so we can recognize it.**
He reveals the pattern of restoration **so we can return to Him.**
He reveals the pattern of Divine Order **so we can walk in it.**

This chapter prepares the ground for the final movement of Book 3:

Conclusion:

Looking back over the decades, I see now that God was not giving me random insights. He was forming a revelation inside me, a revelation about the nature of Divine Order, the danger of disorder, and the hope of restoration. This chapter serves as the bridge between a lifetime of lessons and the clarity God has given for the days ahead. Divine Order is not a new idea. It is an ancient pattern, revealed in Scripture, confirmed in history, reflected in creation, and written on the hearts of those who walk with God. And now, in these last days, the Spirit is calling us to see the pattern clearly, so that we may walk in the order God intended from the beginning.

CHAPTER THIRTEEN

Restoration Begins With Surrender — The Pathway Back to Divine Order

---

> *"Restoration begins not with willpower, but with surrender."*

> "What God restores, He restores thoroughly—beginning with the heart."

Restoration never begins with effort — it starts with surrender.

Every work of God begins with unveiling. We do not start restoration; God begins it by revealing what is out of order.

This is the mercy of God. He exposes disorder not to shame us, but to **heal** us. This chapter reveals how the Spirit restores Divine Order in the heart of the believer, in the community of the church, and eventually in the world at the return of Christ.

The restoration of Divine Order is not a single event; it is a pathway—one that unfolds through Scripture, through surrender, and through the work of the Spirit.

This chapter explains the steps of that pathway and prepares us for the final revelation in Chapter 14.

Restoration Begins With Revelation

Before God restores, He reveals.

He reveals:

1. The disorder within us
2. The deception around us
3. The drift beneath us
4. The patterns that bind us

5.   The lies we have believed
6.   The wounds we have carried
7.   The idols we have protected
8.   The habits we have normalized
9.   The pride we have justified

God begins where we would never start, with **truth**.

Without revelation, restoration is impossible.

Revelation produces clarity.
Clarity produces humility.
Humility opens the door to transformation.

Revelation Leads to Conviction

Conviction is the Spirit's invitation to return to God's order.

Conviction is not guilt.
Conviction is not condemnation.
Conviction is **alignment**.

Guilt says, "You're a failure."
Conviction says, "This is the way—walk in it."
Condemnation says, "You are unworthy."
Conviction says, "You belong to Me."

Conviction is a gift. It is the moment God points to a place in our life and says:

"This no longer reflects Me. Let me restore it."

Conviction Produces Repentance

Repentance is not merely an apology; repentance is a **return**.

In repentance:

Michael A. Kovach
1. The will yields
2. The heart bows
3. The mind shifts
4. The flesh loses ground
5. The Spirit gains authority

Repentance is the moment the believer agrees with God:

"You are right.
Your way is true.
My way leads to disorder.
I return to You."

Repentance is not a punishment; it is an invitation into freedom.

Repentance Produces Purification

Purification is the process through which:

1. Habits change
2. Desires transform
3. Wounds heal
4. Lies break
5. Sin loses its appeal
6. Righteousness becomes natural

Purification is not immediate. It is a refining fire.

The Spirit removes what does not belong while strengthening what does.

Purification is not about perfection; it is about alignment with Divine Order.

Purification Leads to Alignment

Alignment is the stage where:

1. The will agrees with the Spirit
2. The mind is renewed by truth
3. Emotions submit to righteousness

4.   Habits reflect holiness
5.   Relationships reflect Christ
6.   Priorities reflect obedience

Alignment is the fruit of surrender. It is the moment the believer begins to walk in the stability, peace, clarity, and strength that come from living under God's order.

Alignment is the restoration of the inner architecture God designed.

Alignment Produces Empowerment

The Spirit empowers those who walk in alignment.

Empowerment is not emotional intensity; it is spiritual authority.

A believer aligned with Divine Order experiences:

1.   Greater discernment
2.   Deeper peace
3.   Increased clarity
4.   Spiritual strength
5.   Bold obedience
6.   Holy confidence
7.   Stability under pressure
8.   Joy in surrender

Empowerment is not the reward for righteousness; it is the natural result of alignment.

Empowerment Produces Fruitfulness

Fruitfulness is the visible evidence of Divine Order restored.

Fruitfulness is not activity.
It is not busyness.
It is not a religious performance.

Fruitfulness is:

Michael A. Kovach
1. Transformed character
2. Lasting obedience
3. Genuine holiness
4. Love that reflects Christ
5. Peace that surpasses understanding
6. Wisdom rooted in Scripture
7. Courage grounded in truth
8. Relationships shaped by grace
9. Work infused with purpose

Fruitfulness is the life Jesus described in John 15: A life rooted in Him, nourished by Him, and aligned with Him.

Restoration in the Church

What God does in individuals, He does in His people.

The restoration of the church follows the same pathway:

1. **Revelation** - God exposes compromise, deception, and drift.

2. **Conviction** - The church feels the weight of truth.

3. **Repentance** - Leaders and congregations return to biblical fidelity.

4. **Purification** - False teaching, carnal leadership, and cultural compromise are removed.

5. **Alignment** - The church embraces holiness, obedience, and the authority of Scripture.

6. **Empowerment** - The Spirit restores power, unity, and discernment.

7. **Fruitfulness** - The church becomes a light once again—A witness to Christ in a darkening age.

Church renewal is not a new strategy—it is the restoration of Divine Order.

Restoration in the World

This chapter would be incomplete without acknowledging the final movement of Divine Order.

What begins in the believer and expands in the church will culminate in the **return of Christ**, when He restores order to all creation.

Paul writes:

"Creation itself will also be set free from its slavery to corruption."
— Romans 8:21 (NASB95)

This is the final restoration: The restoration of everything. Christ is not coming back to repair the world—He is coming to **restore** it.

The Pattern of Restoration Is God's Signature

The pathway:

1.   Revelation
2.   Conviction
3.   Repentance
4.   Purification
5.   Alignment
6.   Empowerment
7.   Fruitfulness

This is not a formula—it is the fingerprint of God.

Whenever Divine Order is restored, this is the pattern He uses.

It is consistent.
It is ancient.
It is biblical.
It is universal.
It is true.

Conclusion:

Michael A. Kovach

Chapter 13 revealed the pathway of restoration inside the believer and inside the church. It is the movement from disorder to Divine Order—a movement initiated by God, sustained by the Spirit, and embraced through surrender. Chapter 14 prepares us for the culmination of Book 3:

CHAPTER FOURTEEN

The Spirit, the Bride, and the End of All Disorder

"The King is not merely returning—He is restoring everything disorder has touched."

"The Spirit and the Bride do not whisper—they proclaim: 'Come.'"

The final chapter of this trilogy looks forward to the moment when Divine Order is no longer partial, internal, or spiritual, but **universal**.

Daniel foresaw a time when:

"Many of those who sleep in the dust of the earth shall awake,
Some to everlasting life,
Some to shame and everlasting contempt.
Those who are wise shall shine
Like the brightness of the firmament."— Daniel 12:2–3 (NKJV)

Revelation completes the picture:

"The Spirit and the Bride say, 'Come.'"

This chapter weaves together:

- The hope of resurrection.
- The purifying work of the Spirit.
- The preparation of the Bride.
- The final exposure of disorder.
- The return of Jesus.
- The restoration of all things.

Michael A. Kovach

Divine Order does not merely repair the world — it prepares the world for the King.

Every book of Scripture, every covenant, every prophetic whisper, and every movement of God in history points toward one climactic reality: **the restoration of all things under the authority of Christ.** Divine Order is not fully realized in this age; it is moving toward a cosmic fulfillment that only the return of Jesus can bring.

Disorder entered creation through rebellion.
Disorder spread through pride.
Disorder corrupted nations, institutions, families, and hearts.

But disorder is temporary.
Divine Order is eternal.

This chapter reveals the final movement of restoration — the work of the Spirit in the last days, the purification of the Bride, and the return of the King who ends all disorder forever.

The Spirit: Restorer of Order in the Last Days

The Spirit is not passive.
He is preparing the world for Christ's return with increasing intensity.

Joel prophesied:

"I will pour out My Spirit on all flesh." — Joel 2:28 (NKJV)

Peter confirmed its beginning at Pentecost — but the outpouring continues until the end of the age.

The Spirit's work in the last days intensifies:

1.   Convicting the world of sin, righteousness, and judgment (John 16:8, NASB95)

2.   Awakening a slumbering church

3.   Gathering a remnant

4.   Restoring authentic discernment

5.   Exposing deception

6.   Empowering gifts for endurance

7.   Purifying hearts for holiness

8.   Preparing the Bride for her Bridegroom

The Spirit is not withdrawing — He is escalating.

Where disorder multiplies, **the Spirit works most intensely.**

The bride: A People Being Purified for Her King

Scripture reveals a profound truth:

"The marriage of the Lamb has come, and His bride has made herself ready."— Revelation 19:7 (NKJV)

Readiness is not ceremonial — it is transformational.

The Bride makes herself ready through:

1.   Repentance

2.   Obedience

3.   Holiness

4.   Truth embraced without compromise

5.   Rejecting false doctrine

6.   Enduring in faith

7.   Purified love

8.   Joyful submission to Christ

Michael A. Kovach

Readiness is not enthusiasm.

Readiness is alignment with Divine Order.

Jesus warned that many would claim intimacy with Him yet be unknown to Him (Matthew 7:23). The Bride is recognized not by her appearance, but by her likeness — her life bears the image of her King.

The final purification of the church is not punishment — it is preparation.

The Collision of Two Orders

As the kingdom advances, it confronts the disorder of this age.

Jesus told Pilate:

"My kingdom is not of this world."— John 18:36 (NASB95)

Yet His kingdom advances through the lives of believers. And the more the kingdom manifests, the more visible the clash becomes between Divine Order and worldly disorder.

This collision reveals:

1.   The world's hostility to truth

2.   The church's need for discernment

3.   The believer's need for endurance

4.   The exposure of counterfeit religion

5.   The intensification of spiritual warfare

The last days are not the triumph of disorder—they are the **exposure** of disorder before its destruction.

Judgment: The Final Removal of Disorder

Judgment is not cruelty — it is cleansing.

God's judgment removes everything that distorts His design.

Peter writes:

"It is time for judgment to begin with the household of God."
— 1 Peter 4:17 (NASB95)

This judgment purifies:

1.   The church.

2.   The believer.

3.   Doctrine.

4.   Motives.

5.   The inner life.

When Christ returns, judgment expands outward:

1.   Evil destroyed.

2.   Rebellion silenced.

3.   The deception ended.

4.   Darkness dispelled.

5.   Death defeated.

6.   Creation healed.

7.   Nations restored

8.   Righteousness established.

Judgment is not the end of the world. It is the end of disorder.

The Return of the King: Order Restored Universally

Revelation does not depict annihilation — it depicts **renewal**.

Michael A. Kovach

1.	A new heaven.

2.	A new earth.

3.	A healed creation.

4.	A restored humanity.

5.	A reigning King.

6.	A purified Bride.

7.	A world without the curse.

Christ does not merely fix the world — He **recreates** it.

"Behold, I make all things new. "— Revelation 21:5 (NKJV)

When Christ returns:

1.	Righteousness will dwell in the earth (2 Peter 3:13).

2.	Creation will be set free from corruption (Romans 8:21).

3.	Death, mourning, crying, and pain will cease (Revelation 21:4).

4.	Every knee will bow (Philippians 2:10-11).

5.	God will dwell with humanity (Revelation 21:3).

This is the fullness of Divine Order restored.

The Role of the Redeemed in the Coming Kingdom

Every act of obedience in this life prepares believers for responsibility in the kingdom to come.

Scripture reveals that we will:

1.	Reign with Christ (2 Timothy 2:12)

2.	Judge angels (1 Corinthians 6:3)

3.	Carry His glory

4.   Administer His righteousness

5.   Participate in His restoration of creation

Sanctification today prepares you for kingdom responsibility tomorrow.

The Final Harmony: The Spirit and the Bride Speak as One

The ultimate sign of Divine Order is found in Revelation:

"The Spirit and the bride say, 'Come.'" — Revelation 22:17 (NKJV)

This is not sentiment. It is alignment.

The Spirit cries, "Come," because the mission is complete.
The Bride cries, "Come," because her heart is ready.

When the Spirit's desire and the Bride's desire unite,
Divine Order has reached its completion.

The final revival is not emotional frenzy — it is preparation for the King.

Conclusion: The End of Disorder, the Dawn of Order

Everything in Scripture — from Genesis to Revelation — moves toward this moment:

1.   Christ reigning

2.   Creation restored

3.   The Bride purified

4.   Nations healed

5.   Evil destroyed

6.   Divine Order is established forever

Michael A. Kovach
Disorder has an expiration date.
Divine Order does not.

And as we approach the return of Christ, the Spirit is preparing a people who will stand in truth, walk in holiness, endure with courage, and long for the appearing of their King.

This is our hope.
This is our destiny.
This is the end of the old order—and the beginning of the world we were created for.

EPILOGUE

A Final Word to the Reader — Stepping Into the Order You Were Made For

---

"You were created to reflect Divine Order in a world drowning in confusion."

"You belong to the Kingdom that cannot be shaken."

This trilogy concludes not with closure, but with commissioning.

You were created for order, not chaos.
For truth, not confusion.
For alignment, not drift.

This Epilogue reminds the reader that:

- Restoration begins in the heart

- The Spirit is patient and thorough

- The believer carries divine order into a disordered world

- The return of Christ is the great hope anchoring every act of obedience

It ends with the call:

Walk in His order. Live in His truth. Stand in His hope. You belong to the Kingdom that cannot be shaken.

If you've journeyed through all three books of *The Restoration of Divine Order*, then you already know something essential:

You were created for order, not chaos.
For truth, not confusion.

Michael A. Kovach
For alignment, not drift.
For life, not survival.

This trilogy was not written to criticize the world or condemn the church. It was written to shine light on a design woven into creation, revealed in Scripture, validated by history, and confirmed in the heart of every believer who walks with God.

Divine Order is not rigid.
It is not oppressive.
It is not cold or mechanical.
It is the very atmosphere of God's presence—the organizing principle of His kingdom, His nature, and His purpose.

This Epilogue is not a conclusion. It is a commissioning.

1. You Are Part of God's Restoration Story

From Genesis to Revelation, the entire biblical narrative is a story of order → disorder → restoration.

1.   Eden begins with order.

2.   The Fall introduces disorder.

3.   Redemption begins restoration.

4.   The Kingdom completes it.

And right now — in this moment — you stand inside that story.

You are not merely observing the world's disorder.
You are called to embody God's order within it.

This is your inheritance.
This is your responsibility.
This is your privilege.

2. Restoration Begins With You

The Spirit restores order first **within** the believer.

Before God restores society,
Before He restores institutions,
Before He restores nations,

He restores **the heart**.

Your heart.
Your mind.
Your will.
Your relationships.
Your inner architecture.

When Divine Order rules inside you, you carry the kingdom wherever you go.

You become:

1.   A stabilizing presence.

2.   A beacon of truth.

3.   A vessel of peace.

4.   A witness to Christ.

5.   A person who does not collapse under pressure.

You become a living contradiction to a world enslaved by confusion.

3. Do Not Be Discouraged By the Times

It is easy to look at the world and feel overwhelmed:

1.   Moral drift.

2.   Ideological conflict.

3.   Spiritual decline.

4.   Institutional corruption.

Michael A. Kovach

5.　　　Relational fragmentation.

6.　　　Generational confusion.

But God placed you here **on purpose**.

You were not born in the wrong era.
You were born for this one.

Empires fall.
Institutions shake.
Cultures shift.
But the kingdom of God is unshakable.

The darker the age, the clearer the light of Christ shines through His people.

4. Let the Spirit Align What Has Drifted

If any part of your life feels out of order, that is not a sign of failure —it is an invitation.

You don't need to fix yourself.
You need to surrender yourself.

You don't need to be stronger.
You need to be aligned.

You don't need more willpower.
You need more yielding.

The Spirit is patient.
He restores slowly, thoroughly, lovingly, and completely.

Every area you place under His authority will be healed, ordered, and renewed.

5. Hold Fast to the Hope of His Return

The final restoration is still ahead.

One day:

1. Righteousness will dwell permanently
2. Creation will be healed
3. The curse will be removed
4. The Bride will be perfected
5. Evil will be abolished
6. Nations will be restored
7. Tears will be wiped away
8. Wars will cease
9. And Christ will reign

This hope is not escapism. It is expectation — the expectation of a world restored to the order God intended from the beginning.

Let this hope anchor you when the world trembles.

6. A Final Charge

As you close this trilogy, carry this truth with you:

Wherever Divine Order is restored, Christ is revealed.

In your life.
In your relationships.
In your home.
In your church.
In your workplace.
In your community.
In your decisions.
In your thoughts.
In your obedience.

Michael A. Kovach

You were created to reflect the order of God in a disordered world.
You were created to carry His presence.
You were created to walk in His design.
You were created to display His kingdom.

And the Spirit is with you — guiding, convicting, strengthening, aligning,
and preparing you for the day when the King returns to restore all things.

Until that day,
walk in His order.
Live in His truth.
Stand in His hope.
Rest in His peace.
And never forget:

You belong to the Kingdom that cannot be shaken.

DOCTRINAL GUARDRAIL

A Framework for Testing Ideas, Interpretations, and Spiritual Impressions

---

The purpose of this checklist is to help believers discern whether a teaching, impression, interpretation, or "new insight" is truly from God or merely the product of emotion, culture, or personal preference. These guardrails protect against drift, deception, and disordered interpretations of Scripture.

Use these questions prayerfully, humbly, and honestly.

1. Does it align with the whole counsel of Scripture?

A truth cannot contradict Scripture anywhere — not in pattern, principle, or implication.
The Spirit never reveals something that opposes the Word He inspired.

2. Does it affirm the deity, lordship, and supremacy of Jesus Christ?

If a belief minimizes Christ, shifts attention away from Him, or redefines Him, it is not from God.

3. Does it agree with the historic faith "once delivered to the saints"? (Jude 3)

Orthodoxy is a safety fence, not a restriction.
God does not "update" the gospel to fit modern culture.

4. Does it lead the believer toward holiness, obedience, and repentance?

Michael A. Kovach

Truth transforms.

Error excuses.

If an idea justifies sin or removes the call to obedience, it is not from the Spirit.

5. Does it require humility, or does it flatter pride?

The Spirit leads us downward into surrender.
The flesh leads us upward into self-exaltation.

6. Does it elevate Scripture above emotion, experience, or preference?

Truth is not shaped by what we feel.
Truth shapes what we feel.

7. Does it produce the fruit of the Spirit? (Galatians 5:22–23)

Love, joy, peace, patience, kindness, goodness, faithfulness, gentleness, self-control.
If the fruit is absent, the root is suspect.

8. Does it withstand correction from mature believers?

A truth that cannot be questioned is a truth that should be questioned.

9. Does it withstand time, pressure, and testing?

Truth remains true even when circumstances change.
Counterfeits collapse under pressure.

10. Does it glorify God rather than man?

If the center shifts from Christ to self — even subtly — disorder has entered.

✔ A Final Guardrail Word

The Spirit will never lead where Scripture forbids, never reveal what Scripture denies, never contradict what Christ established, and never affirm what God calls sin.

Truth is not a moving target.
It is a Person — and His name is Jesus.

Michael A. Kovach

ORTHODOX FOUNDATIONS NOTES

Core Doctrines Anchoring the Theology of Divine Order

These notes summarize the essential biblical doctrines assumed throughout the trilogy. They serve as a theological anchor and a point of clarity for any reader seeking to understand the foundations beneath the arguments presented in Book 3.

1. The Nature of God

God is holy, sovereign, eternal, and unchanging.
Divine Order flows from His nature — not human invention.
(Exodus 3:14; Isaiah 6:3; Malachi 3:6)

2. The Authority of Scripture

Scripture is the inspired, infallible, and sufficient Word of God — the standard by which all truth claims must be tested.
(2 Timothy 3:16–17; Psalm 119:89)

3. The Depravity of Man

Humanity has fallen, is disordered, and powerless to restore itself.
Restoration requires divine intervention, not human effort.
(Genesis 3; Romans 3:23)

4. The Person and Work of Jesus Christ

Jesus is fully God and fully man; His life, death, resurrection, and ascension are the center of Divine Order and redemption.
(John 1:1–14; 1 Corinthians 15:3–4)

5. The Indwelling and Empowering of the Holy Spirit

The Spirit regenerates, convicts, sanctifies, guides, illuminates, strengthens, and prepares the believer for the return of Christ.
(John 16:13; Romans 8:9–16)

6. Salvation by Grace Through Faith

Salvation is God's work from beginning to end — received through faith, secured by grace, and evidenced by transformation.
(Ephesians 2:8–10)

7. The Church as Christ's Body

The Church exists to proclaim the gospel, make disciples, and manifest the kingdom of God. Disorder enters when it departs from this mission.
(Ephesians 4:11–16)

8. Sanctification as Spirit-Led Transformation

The believer grows in holiness not by willpower but by surrender, obedience, and the Spirit's work within.
(Galatians 5:16–25; Romans 8)

9. The Coming Return of Jesus Christ

Christ will return bodily, visibly, and victoriously to judge the nations, restore creation, and reign forever.
(Acts 1:11; Revelation 19–22)

10. The Final Restoration of All Things

Disorder will end.
Divine Order will be universal.
Every wrong will be made right.
Every tear wiped away.

Michael A. Kovach
Every shadow dispelled.
(Revelation 21:1–5)

Study Notes

Michael A. Kovach